CHOICE FOR NOWHERE MEN

CHOICE FOR NOWHERE MEN

A look at Humanism and Christianity

by Joan Wragg, B.A., Ph.D.

SCRIPTURE UNION
5 Wigmore Street, London, W.1

© Joan Wragg 1969

First published 1969

SBN 85421 204 3

Printed in Great Britain
by Billing & Sons Limited, Guildford and London

Contents

Chapter 1

'I think I'm a Humanist'

'What's a Humanist?'

Dave looked more thoughtful than usual. He'd just left school—and left the Church too, for that matter. He definitely considered that the time had come to make the break. After all, he was 18. And he'd never cared much for the Church. He'd paraded with the 10th Company of the Brigade for years—every Sunday morning, without fail. But he'd had enough. . . . And as for all this business about God—who's *God* anyway? When some Russian astronaut comes back and says he's seen Him, all right. There'll be a sudden rush on 'L' plates for space craft. . . .

But it can't happen. Nobody seriously believes in God nowadays. The Church is just a place for people who can't think for themselves. . . .

Carol, his sister, wasn't much help this time. She was a Christian. She believed in God without questioning. Nobody could accuse Carol of defying the Almighty. It would never occur to her to dare to. She prayed, read her Bible, and tried to live a good life. In fact she even went to Church if it rained. But, as Dave had guessed, Carol's thinking was somewhat limited.

She looked up. 'What makes *you* suddenly ask what a Humanist is?'

'Because,' said Dave, 'I think I am one.'

And Carol had to let him think it, because she didn't know what a 'Humanist' was, either. Must be a phase he's going through. Best let him sort himself out. . . .

There are plenty of Daves in the world. People with serious doubts about their traditional beliefs. People for whom the Church has become obsolete, meaningless. They realize it would be dishonest to call themselves Christians, so they search around for some other suitable label. At one time they would have been content to remain 'agnostic' or 'atheist' (sometimes meaning 'I don't know' or 'I don't believe in God', but more often simply 'I can't be bothered thinking very deeply about religion. . . .').

Today, however, this is far too negative and unconvincing. If you're not a Christian, you should at least be something else that's positive. And Dave was coming to realize that Humanism offers something very positive. And it's as well for him to investigate it thoroughly before casually announcing this as his new-found allegiance.

Of course, Dave didn't yet know very much about the British Humanist Association. Even in this small, influential group of highly educated, well-read people, there is a variety of opinion and emphasis. The very nature of Humanist philosophy allows this. But apart from the Humanists who have a carefully thought out system, there are many people who, like Dave, have woken up to the fact that God doesn't matter any more for them, and their thinking reflects a more popular Humanism which is very widespread.

There are plenty of Carols in the world, too. Enjoying the security of the 'faith of our fathers', wearing her best coat on Sundays, and teaching every week in the Sunday School, Carol is quite healthy enough while her head is firmly buried in the sand. Cosy, too. But if anyone digs anywhere near and uproots her she'll die of sudden exposure.

And the Humanists are digging, deep into the morass of our ecclesiastical garbage. (And for the Carols of this life, there will be little left to cling to.) They are digging trenches into the traditions which have governed our national and social life for centuries. Britain might have been a Christian country once, they say, but it's an illusion to think it is so any longer. So they advocate changes in the law, and in our schools, changes which could profoundly affect each one of us. Is Humanism receiving respect because it is now the only logical step for a rational being? Or is it because some of us are afraid of wielding the spade of hard thinking?

A survey was conducted recently in three types of secondary school in a Midlands town. It showed that most sixth formers had some idea of

Humanist belief. This must please the teacher as much as it pleases the British Humanist Association, because a few years ago it just wouldn't have been true. Humanists *are* making their presence felt, and are extending their areas of influence. And although we do not here wish to attempt a profound, intellectual reply to an intellectual movement, it is right that we should investigate the effects of the Humanist system of belief upon life for ourselves.

'A Humanist recognizes the rights of every human being, but does not cry out about God the whole time', wrote one sixth former. This, she reckoned, was a good thing. So—has the time come to stop crying out about God? Or is He still worth a hearing?

Is Jesus Christ the way to God, the truth about God and life itself, as He claimed—or is it all a lot of wishful thinking on the part of His security-loving followers?

Has man come of age? Can he do without God now? Is the idea of God merely a comfortable extra for the weak and insecure, but unacceptable to the honest and mature thinker?

Chapter 2

Me to help me?

The philosophers had never had it so good. They meditated about man and the universe, about life and death . . . and groups like the Epicureans staunchly believed that this life was all. 'Eat, drink and be merry, for tomorrow we die,' was their slogan. So they did.

There were still plenty of gods around, though, and plenty of inclination to worship them. When Paul arrived on the scene, he even found an altar 'to the unknown god', just in case any benign deity was left unpraised by mortal man, or an angry one left to stew in his wrath. This was Athens in the first century A.D.

And still the philosophers philosophize, and the poets muse. Still men say 'there is no God', and still people worship Him. The age-old debate goes on. Life has always been and will always be an enigma for some.

'All go to one place; all are from the dust, and all turn to dust again.' That sounds gloomy—if it's true. And surprisingly, it is found not in the works of the Greek philosophers, not in the writings of twentieth-century Humanists, but in the Old Testament itself, in the book of Ecclesiastes. 'Who knows', it goes on, 'whether the spirit of man goes upward and the spirit of the beast goes down to the earth? So I saw that there is nothing better than that a man should enjoy his work, for that is his lot.'

What is life all about? What is the point of it all? Is there a purpose in existence, or is time in fact a wheel, not a road? Dave and Carol find they have different answers to these questions. So have Humanists and Christians.

It has been suggested that in Ecclesiastes, in the Old Testament itself, lie the seeds of Humanist thought. And although in a later chapter, the writer of Ecclesiastes does in fact express a positive hope and belief in God, at this stage he is only re-echoing the despair which so often characterizes different stages in a man's struggle to belief in himself and in God. This is where we start asking ourselves 'What is the point of life?' And some travel along the road to Humanism, and others, working from the same basic starting-point, arrive eventually at Christianity and belief in God.

The fifteenth century was far removed in time from the days of the writer of Ecclesiastes. But it shared the same basic characteristic, namely an eagerness to enquire into life, and a quest for truth. This was the time of the Renaissance, the rebirth of scholarship which inevitably profoundly affected man's views on religion. Beginning in

Italy, this craze for the 'new learning' spread across the Continent to Great Britain. No longer were the Church's edicts blindly accepted. The thinkers stopped to ask 'Why?', and this revolutionized their whole approach to religion. Sincere churchmen like Erasmus and Reuchlin looked for the reform of the religious life of their day. The Church had long been ruled by traditionalism, but now its scholars welcomed the release of the mind from the rut into which it had sunk. There was a desire to read the Old Testament in Hebrew, the New Testament in Greek, and to uncover the pearls of their faith which had been hidden from view by centuries of ecclesiastical lore. Human life took on new value. 'All this and heaven too'—so let's make the most of 'All this'. This was the new Humanism. But it was nevertheless, at this stage, Christianity. A Christian Humanism; for there is still 'heaven too'.

So from the same basic starting-point of new enquiry, in the fifteenth century there developed Humanist belief, and a reformed Church—today poles apart, but once working hand in hand in the search for truth.

Unlike the Renaissance Humanists, modern Humanists are atheists, or certainly agnostics. This is made quite clear in the leaflet produced by the British Humanist Association: 'We find the idea of life after death a monumental piece of wishful thinking . . . we do not believe in God'. And even though all BHA members may not stand by all that the pamphlet says, their attitude is far removed from that of Erasmus and his school. Something must have happened in between, somehow!

Erasmus and his followers started from the premise that 'man is datum', and they moved from there to discuss his relationship to God. Modern secularist Humanism, however, says that 'man is the *only* datum', hence there is no point in going on to consider God.

A Humanism which rejects God became acceptable in the nineteenth century. Darwin's 'theory of evolution' knocked most religious thinkers for six, because the Church was not ready for the findings of this kind of scientific research. Darwin himself was not a Humanist. His *Origin of Species*, however, became the origin of a conflict out of which arose the school of scientific Humanists, with Thomas Henry Huxley as one of its key exponents. It is not surprising that with all the progress and developments which revolutionized the scientific and industrial world, affecting people as they sat in their homes, this new thinking had its appeal.

> 'O man . . . when I consider the work of thy fingers
> What is God that thou art mindful of Him?'

Christian Humanism was to give way to a religion of humanity. And the two aren't the same. Worship of Almighty God was being replaced by worship of Almighty man. After all, 'man possesses boundless capacity for self-improvement', said J. H. Breasted in America. And he was only echoing the ideas of people like Auguste Comte and Ernest Renan on the Continent, or Gilbert Murray in Britain.

So in the 1890s two societies, the Ethical Union and the Rationalist Press Association, were founded. It is only recently that these were amalgamated to form the British Humanist Association.

The atheistic position of the modern Humanist, then, is the result of a gradual development of ideas. But even since the turn of the century the meaning of the term 'Humanist' has altered. Today, 'to describe someone as a Humanist', says Margaret Knight, 'does not usually imply that he has been educated in *litterae humaniores*. Rather it implies that he sees no reason for believing in a supernatural God, or in a life after death; that he holds that man must face his problems with his own intellectual and moral resources, without invoking supernatural aid, and that authority, supernatural or otherwise should not be allowed to obstruct inquiry in any field of thought' (*Humanist Anthology*, Intro., p. 13).

A positive atheism. A militant Humanism. We shall look at the basic assumptions of modern Humanism against this background. It's one thing to say 'I don't believe in God', but this leaves man on his own. So where do we go from there? Already we are realizing that it's not enough for

Dave simply to declare that he thinks he's a Humanist, or for Carol to shut her mind to the existence of Humanism merely because it's easier that way. Humanism, like Christianity, affects life. And Humanism, like Christianity, demands commitment of mind as well as of feelings.

Chapter 3

Prove God exists!

'Prepare to meet thy God.' The message of the greying whitewash on the embankment house is a timely one. Charging through the countryside at 100 m.p.h., whistling through the signals which govern not only your destination but, at this rate, probably your destiny as well, is as good a time as any to prepare to meet one's God. That is—if there is a God, or ever was one.

'God is dead.' We don't read it on placards or wayside pulpits, but Humanists shout this slogan just as loudly. And although it is cold comfort if you feel you're about to join Him any minute now, most people in fact prefer this message. At least— they live as though they do, and their insistent retort, 'Of course I believe in God' doesn't really mean anything at all.

If there's one thing that annoys Dave, it's this 'I believe in God' business. He's always on at Carol about it.

'All right,' he says, 'You're so sure God exists— prove it.'

Involuntarily inarticulate, Carol 'well's' and

11

'you know's' until she remembers at least one thing worth saying.

'There must have been someone to start all this lot off. Be reasonable!'

'I *am* being reasonable.' Yes, there was nobody more reasonable than Dave. So Dave thought.

'Well, how else can we be here? I mean—there must have been a beginning,' continued Carol.

'Of course there must have been a beginning. But that doesn't prove that God was there.'

'Well, it does. I mean, it says so. So it must do, I mean . . .'

Dave slammed his book down. 'For goodness sake, Carol, what do you mean? *It* says so. *Who* says so? The Bible? You'll tell me Adam and Eve were in the garden in their fig leaves next. Honestly, Carol, it makes me sick the way you swallow everything they tell you at that church of yours.'

Carol shuffled uneasily. She wasn't much of a debater. She thought it all a bit unnecessary really. Anyway, what if she had missed that science survey about the Neolithic Age on television last night? Their vicar said science hadn't got all the answers. The Genesis story couldn't just be ignored. After all, it was in the Bible, wasn't it?

*   *   *

In the Bible. The year 4004 B.C. That's when it

all began. God said, 'Let there be light' and there was light. God created man in His own image. And Eve gave Adam the apple. It all happened in the year 4004 B.C. It must be true. An Archbishop had calculated the date, and on his authority, Bible margins stated it, and the people believed it. Nobody could argue with the Archbishop. . . .

Until, one day, along came Charles Darwin. At least, he'd been around for some time, trapesing around South America in the *Beagle*, observing fossils and land structures, plants and animals. A happy and unforeseen consequence of his association at Cambridge—to which seat of learning he had gone with the intention of becoming a clergyman. Darwin's study of the theories of Lamarck, which had been largely disregarded by the general public, and even scientists, led him to suspect that there might be a grain of truth in the theory of an evolutionary development of man. Lamarck had very firmly believed in environmental selection. That is, a giraffe has a long neck because its particular function and territory require it, not because God looked on His world and thought 'Let there be a giraffe with a long neck to add a bit of variety on the landscape'.

Lamarck presented his theories two generations before Darwin's findings. But few people took any notice. Any changes observable in the structure and life of the earth since the creation are entirely due to the Flood of Noah's day.

'The Lord looked down from His window in the sky
and said, I created man, but I don't remember why.
Nothing but fighting since Creation Day
So I'll send a little water and wash them all away.'

So the world of the last century was believed to
be the result of that 'water'.

Creation Day? Darwin's reading of Lamarck,
and his own studies of Natural Science, led him to
question this long-held concept of the instantaneous creation of the world, at a moment of
time. He didn't throw God out of the picture; he
wasn't concerned with proving or disproving His
existence. But in 1859, sure of his findings, he
presented them, carefully tabulated, in his *Origin
of Species*, by means of Natural selection or the
preservation of Favoured Races in the struggle for
life. This was followed in 1871 by his publication
called *The Descent of Man, and selection in relation to
sex*.

His views differed from Lamarck's slightly but,
for the general opinion, drastically. The damage
was done. There was no documented evidence to
support the theory of instantaneous creation.
Genesis stood alone. And people were not ready
for a challenger. No one, except the Thomas
Henry Huxleys of the day, wanted to side with the
challenger. It was much nicer to feel secure in the
blessed thought that one is made in the image of
God, rather than that there are innumerable apes
and other mammals and amphibians along the line
of our evolutionary development. The more

unsure the country parsons felt, the more vehemently they attacked this new blasphemy from their pulpits. There were those whose faith was completely shattered: no instantaneous creation—no Genesis—no God—no heaven. Hope was replaced by despair. There were others who closed their minds to this new intrusion, finding their bliss in ignorance. There were others who managed to think their position through, bearing in mind their theology and the new scientific findings.

Was there no room for God now? Had Darwin got rid of Him, once for all? Napoleon once asked Laplace where God was in his theories of astronomy. 'Sir,' came the reply, 'I have no need of that hypothesis.' Yet Laplace was a practising Christian. Similarly if Darwin had been asked where God was in his theories of the development of man, he might well have given the same answer. For Darwin was not disproving, ignoring or rejecting God. He was just examining the world He had made. Darwin, too, was a practising churchman. No, he had not got rid of God, once for all.

You might be asking, 'What has all this to do with Humanism?' The basic tenet of Humanism is that of evolutionary change. Disprove this, and Humanism collapses. For man, believes the Humanist, not only owes his present existence to a long and gradual evolutionary process, but also his future happiness, too, since he must still be evolving and will one day achieve a more perfect society in which to live.

Does it surprise you that now, 100 years after Darwin, the Humanists haven't won the day? That, in fact, although there are many Carols in the Church, there are also many thinking Christians—scientists, philosophers, surgeons and professors, who remain convinced and practising Christians, despite all the pressures from those who advocate atheism as the only tenable position for the honest intellectual? Dave thought he was being reasonable when he said that you couldn't prove the existence of God. Carol thought it equally reasonable to try to argue that the only answer to the enigma of life is God. They couldn't both be right. Or could they?

Many non-Christians, like Dave, agree with Bertrand Russell when he said, 'What really moves people to believe in God is not any intellectual argument at all. Most people believe in God because they have been taught from early infancy to do it.' Christians would shout a loud 'yes' to the first part of this statement. It was generally much more than intellectual argument that moved them to faith. But the fact that many depart from church and belief after a careful schooling in infancy in the doctrines of the Christian faith, together with the fact that others come to a sure belief in God after years of agnosticism or even atheism, denies that one's faith is merely attributable to teaching received 'from early infancy'.

If Carol had been more acquainted with the intellectual arguments for the existence of God, she could have answered Dave like this: if there is any sort of mind behind the universe, an all-perfect being whom we call God, the fact of His existence must be included among His attributes, otherwise He would cease to be all-perfect. We exist, so if there is anyone beyond ourselves, He must at least *exist* also.

Or that, as every event must have a cause, the only sufficient cause for the creation of an event as vast as the universe must be God. In other words, if we keep going back far enough along the line of history, we eventually meet an uncaused cause, where there is nothing beyond. This is what we call God. He must exist and be the cause of all that exists.

Or Carol could have said that the design and order of the universe must be the work of a master craftsman and designer. And this must be God.

These three traditional arguments for the existence of God are called the ontological, cosmological and teleological arguments, respectively. They do not in themselves prove the existence of God. At least, whatever effect they may have on you, I have to admit that they don't convince me that He's there. The mind boggles, as they say, when it sets itself the task of reasoning

17

everything out, of imagining what the beginning of things was like, or the end, or space, time and nothingness. But these arguments have their value in demonstrating that there is no easy answer, no quick formula; and that when Lamarck, Darwin, T. H. Huxley and Bertrand Russell have had their say, God may in fact still be there, listening in.

The Humanist philosophy, then, is based on the theory of evolutionary change, with no God in sight, either at the beginning or the end of things. We have evolved from apes anonymous. We will progress to perfect man—or could do, given suitable conditions. Huxley has said, 'The primacy of human personality is a *postulate* of Christianity, and of liberal democracy; but it is a fact of evolution. By whatever objective standard we choose to take, properly developed human personalities are the highest products of evolution.' The ancient poet said that man is the measure of all things.

Now this, though a Humanist tenet, is no less a Christian one. The only difference is that we don't look to the future for properly developed human personality. We look to Jesus Christ, and we believe that He who said 'Be perfect, as your Father in heaven is perfect' (the Greek word means fully developed, mature, complete . . .) can in fact produce this kind of maturity in a person in any age, depending on that person's response to Him. The Biblical writer meant this when he said,

'God created man in His own image'. Man—the highest form of creation. And there is no need to exclude God from the scene whether you accept Darwin or Genesis, or any other theory. In fact, He won't be excluded.

Dave thinks about things quite a bit. What if the Genesis account isn't true? Then Carol hasn't a leg to stand on. The ground is completely gone from under her feet. As Humanists rest their philosophy on the evolutionary theory, so Christians rest their faith on the Genesis account. At least, that's what Dave thinks.

But people like Dave forget some very important points about Genesis chapter 1. They expect a scientific explanation, when what we find in Genesis 1 is really a theological statement about the fact that God actually did start all this lot off, as Carol had thought, and that man and woman are made in the divine image; and that there was estrangement from God in the earliest days. The more ambitious of such critics look for a chronological account in Genesis, and try to correlate it with scientific findings, whereas what Genesis really contains is a logical interpretation of the creation of the known world in terms of the culture of the times. There is more than one way of writing history. And in any record the historian is going to be selective in the material he includes. Is Genesis chapter 1 history? Because God is affirmed to be the cause and creator of the Universe, the answer is yes. The writer of the account does not say *how* God did everything. He is satisfied to know that He did. Thus any concept of a purely naturalistic evolution, without God, is ruled out for the Christian, whatever might be his pet idea of how Genesis should be interpreted. Don't forget, though, that no scientist has yet proved that there wasn't a Mr. and Mrs. Adam, or that they weren't the first couple on earth. And that's a thought, for what it's worth.

No complete answer has been found to account fully for man's existence here on earth. The Christian believes that he is the handiwork of God, the omniscient and omnipotent Creator. The Humanist believes he has evolved by some inexplicable coincidence, without God. The Bible says why we were created. The scientist attempts to show how. The two explanations are complementary rather than contradictory. But if God exists, this affects our present life, for His laws must be taken into account, and He must be respected in our actions and thoughts. It also affects our future life. For if there is a God, there is immortality, there is heaven. No God, no heaven. Death is the end.

When I ring up a secretary at work, I don't debate the likelihood of her existence, even though I can't see her. I know she's there because I recognize her voice and because work which I send in hand-written comes back typed. So, when a person has talked with God, and met Him, even though he can't see Him, he ceases to argue any more, but now behaves as though He's there. It is a two-way relationship, as it is between myself and the secretary. When our requests are made known to God, we do receive an answer. We find God's characteristics and attributes reliable when we put into practice and faith what we read in the Bible . . . and thus we experience God's presence. And it is then that we feel it would be worth Dave's risk, and the risk of others like him, to 'try' God, humbly and sincerely, some time. Because many who openly deny the existence of God have never, in fact, personally experienced His presence, never put Him to the test, as it were, expecting a result. In fact they have never taken Him at His word.

Now it could be said that no existence can be proved. *Cogito, ergo sum*, said Descartes. *I think, therefore I am*. I can't prove that it is so. If I speak to you and you answer me, I presume that both I and you exist. I believe, you believe it. Why? Because we have reacted to each other as we would have expected, according to known law and the habits of man. But how am I to set about *proving* to anyone that I exist? What language would I use? I can only speak about things within my experience. But what if it is all an illusion, one great hoax, a dream, a figment of the imagination?

In the same way it is impossible to prove or disprove God by intellectual argument. And yet Christians claim not only that He exists but that they know Him, and He knows them. One could argue that we are now talking about questions of belief, and that belief is a matter of personal taste and choice. Of course this is a question of belief. But no more so than the matter of whether Descartes exists, or myself. The Christian believes God exists because He acts according to known laws, because He has established contact with man through Jesus Christ, and when the Christian takes Him at His word and prays, he knows answers to his prayers; when he asks for forgiveness, he knows that he receives it and its attendant peace of mind. Some would say it is dangerous to speak of subjective experiences, as no two experiences are likely to be identical. Somewhere or other we need objective facts, and these we have in the life story of Jesus Christ. But more of this later. . . .

Why do I accept the fact of my own existence? Why do I ignore the philosopher who says, 'It's all in the mind, you know'? Because I am all too aware that I have a life to live, work to do, a part to play in my own environment. I have power to love deeply, hate cruelly; I can throb with enthusiasm or I can scream and tear my hair out; I can submit, I can rebel; I can live, I can die. So if someone comes along and challenges the fact of my existence, I want to know what solution he has found to my feeling all this without 'being'. There is no other answer.

Is God 'all in the mind'? Sometimes it would be

easier to think so, because then we could escape His demands. But the answer to life would elude us at the same time, and an existence would have no backbone, no muscle, and would be nothing more than an option for the deluded.

They are like the boy who looks at his cot smothered in Christmas presents and ignores them, saying he can't believe they're for him, that as far as he can see there is no reason why they should be there. So he won't accept them, but carries on as though he'd never seen them. There is more to Christianity than this, of course. It follows that if God does exist, that if the Genesis account is recording great theological truths, and God has made us for Himself, then He will make some demands. It does cost something—everything, in fact. And like the teenager who rebels against parental 'interference' with his affairs, and leaves home to live it up in a flat . . . many people walk out on the whole business. Dave, for instance, says he's tried Church and it doesn't work. But that is not the same as trying God, and it should be Carol's next move to tell him so. But more of this later. . . .

*   *   *

Have you ever been out in the hills in the snow? The melting icicles on the hedgerows drip, drip softly on to the covered earth; the trees, filigree white, pose majestic in the stillness before our gaze; the virgin fields glisten in the pale January sunshine. You forget your cold feet, your hob-nailed boots, your rucksack gnawing at your shoulders. Suddenly you become aware of something beyond yourself, something spiritual. . . .

There is a sense in which one's spiritual perception is stimulated by beauty. Perhaps you yourself hate the countryside. But you like art, music, poetry, or you like design or fashion, or the satisfaction of producing a good piece of work. . . . You become aware of an aesthetic sense. There is more to life than flesh and blood. There is personality. There is spirit. There is something infinite, immortal. . . . Yes, we all feel it from time to time. Keats put it this way:

> 'Beauty is truth, truth beauty;—that is all
> Ye know on earth, and all ye need know.'
> *(from Ode on a Grecian Urn)*

To look at beauty and see beauty alone is impossible. It is a pointer to truth, to God.

Why do we talk like this? Because the Humanist says, I have evolved to my present state through many stages of the evolutionary process. I don't know where I came from, but it wasn't God. It can't have been God. I don't really know where I'm going, but that isn't God, either. All power is given unto me. I can mould my present. I can govern my future. It all depends on me. . . .

The Christian, however, can show him graveyards and cemeteries full of indispensable people.

He says, I came from God, I go to God, and God is in charge of my life. The world is God's and its beauty, and I can give my life to Him. He has the key to the meaning of life and its purpose. It is, in fact, possible to know the infinite, the immortal, whose spiritual presence we felt in the grandeur and the stillness of the countryside. Jesus Christ said, 'I am the way, the truth and the life; no one comes to the Father (God) but by Me' (John 14.6). Those who heed His words are not marching on to an elusive Utopia. They have in fact arrived already.

Darwin or Genesis, then? We might risk offending one or two ardent defenders of the Genesis account who haven't yet forgiven Darwin, by saying it doesn't really matter, since neither exclude God. And God could in fact have used the process of evolution as a tool to prepare the world for man. But while Humanists are content when the evolutionary account has been given and see no further questions to ask, Christians want to probe still further back, and ask what happened before there was anything to evolve. Where did the original 'bits' come from, and how did it all work out? 'Some call it evolution, others call it God. . . .' Others call it God and evolution. So Christians look to God as the maker and sustainer of the universe, while the Humanist philosophy is founded on the idea of Evolution with a capital E. But 'Evolution' as a mystic something that gets things done, is really rather a superstitious notion and is in fact no foundation at all; it provides no basis for living, no hope for the future of man, and no workable solution to the problem of daily living.

Chapter 4

Permissive is the password

'A real Christian, that's what I call him. Never did a soul any harm, and I've never heard him utter an unkind word all the years I've known him. In fact, a finer Christian gentleman I've never met, than old Mr. Shaw.'

'Oh, Mother, you do go on,' said Dave. 'Fine maybe, kind maybe, but not Christian. He'd never call himself a Christian. Why, he's never darkened the doors of a church in years.'

But it wasn't worth going into it all again. Of course it was possible to be a Christian and never grace the ecclesiastical porch with your presence. But it was unlikely. And anyway, Dave knew what Mr. Shaw thought about religion. It's true he was good-natured—kind to the kids, and very good to his family, and the people next door when they had all that trouble.

Dave also knew what his mother meant. She didn't mean 'Christian' really. Anybody she liked, and who was reasonably polite, thoughtful and helpful, she called a 'real Christian'. It was just one of her phrases. She didn't mean it really. But it annoyed Dave all the same. After all, he tried to live a fairly decent kind of life himself, and will be persecuted for evermore by the gang, for breaking with them when they did that job on the jewellers the other week. He didn't see much sense in breaking into places. And he didn't care for the gang. One more feather in his cap. But, please, nobody call him a Christian. That he was not, and had no desire to be. At least, not at the moment, thank you.

For once Carol shared his opinion, because the term 'Christian' bandied about for all and sundry good people annoyed her, too. Morals and religion. The same thing, it seemed, for Mrs. Harvey, like so many people living off their heritage of having been 'born in a Christian country', with a background of dusty Sunday Schools and faithful scholars dutifully uttering the hymn-writer's expression of paradise, 'Above the bright blue sky'. Mrs. Harvey believed not only that the Christian life was a good one, but also that a good life must therefore be a Christian one. But Carol insisted that Christianity was much more than that.

How is it that 'goodness' has come to be equated with Christianity, in the mind of the Englishman, particularly in former generations? One reason is that the Christian life is his ideal. Jesus Christ's teaching is generally revered—even by Humanists. The Lord's Prayer is repeated from early childhood in school assemblies. The Sermon on the Mount, though not often read all through, and even less often studied and applied, is considered, nevertheless, as the theory for the good life.

It is not fashionable to say we live in a Christian country. Neither preacher nor philosopher would say so. But to a certain extent, it is true. In one sense, it is impossible to speak of a country as 'Christian', Christianity being, above all, a personal affair. But were it not for the fact that many of the policies of the Throne and Parliament are governed by Christian traditions and beliefs, the Humanists would have nothing to fight.

How is it that Christianity has come to mean little more than 'goodness'? Because 'goodness' is one of the few concepts which has outlived the idea of a personal God and divine Christ in the thinking of too many churchmen today. In other words, although many preachers no longer 'proclaim Christ', as the Apostles did (see 1 Corinthians 1.17–29) they do proclaim 'goodness and love'. This is supposed to be more 'relevant' nowadays. We are generalizing, of course. But it is sadly true that it is possible to go to a church and hear nothing said about Jesus Christ, who He was, what He did and why, but only to be exhorted pallidly to lead a good life. Herein lies a tragedy. And Christians should mourn the death of life in so many churches. Christianity, as we shall see, is so much more than good living.

And so is Humanism. Much more. This blind acceptance of the label 'Christianity' tagged on to any old good life, is deplored by both Christians and Humanists alike. One leading Humanist, Kingsley Martin, has said: 'I do not believe that morality depends on belief in any set of theological doctrines; it is statistically true that people do not behave better because they hold long-established doctrines.' Who are we to argue with the statistics? In fact, all we are saying is that there are perfectly kind people known to us who, like Mr. Shaw, never go to church—wouldn't if invited—and who would certainly not allow themselves to be called Christian.

*　　*　　*

The war in Vietnam wasn't getting any easier. Television reports didn't make for comfort. Quite the opposite. Yet Dave felt fairly inadequate, curled up in an armchair sipping percolated coffee behind the *Evening News*, many miles from the scene.

'Did you read about those chaps going out to help look after refugees in one of the camps?' asked Dave. 'I really admire that kind of thing. In fact, I wouldn't have minded going myself, if I thought I'd be any use.'

'Nor would I,' said Carol. '. . . not that I'd be much good, I suppose. But it certainly makes you wish you could do something.'

'I don't see why you should want to go.' Dave was wearing his argumentative, I've-left-school-and-know-it-all look again. 'I mean, if we're all going to heaven anyway, wherever that might be, why spend all your energies helping people on earth?'

'We're not all going to heaven anyway. Well, at least, not necessarily.' Carol was indignant. Of course she wanted to help. Jesus helped people, didn't He? And He clearly said we should do the same. 'Love one another.' She recalled the words 'Love one another, as I have loved you' (John 15.12). She was sorting it all out in her mind. She'd never really thought of it much before. She looked at Dave. 'Well, and why do you want to go?'

'Because,' said Dave, 'I believe in trying to help people all we can. I know it sounds horribly do-goodish, coming from me, but there's too much talk and too little action when it comes to giving a helping hand.'

'Well then, I agree,' replied Carol. 'So what are we arguing about? I don't suppose either of us will go in the end.'

Neither of them did go, as it happened. But they were mistaken to suppose that they were arguing about nothing, because the principle involved is one of the basic differences between Christian and Humanist thinking in the field of ethics. 'You ought because you ought,' says the Humanist. 'You ought because God says so,' says the Christian. 'Man is responsible to man,' says the Humanist. 'Man is responsible to God and man,' says the Christian.

'Humanism for the individual is concerned with the art of living,' says Barbara Smoker, a Humanist. 'At the same time Humanism is concerned with the welfare of all, and recognizes that each of us is morally responsible not only for his own personal conduct but also for all behaviour.'

Jesus Christ said, 'A new commandment I give to you, that you love one another, even as I have loved you, that you also love one another. By this all men will know that you are My disciples, if you have love for one another' (John 13.34–35).

There are many points concerned with the 'art of living' on which Humanists and Christians agree. Dave and Carol voiced some of them: both felt an urge to help people in need; both felt their social conscience aroused by human tragedy—in this case, the result of war; both knew they were right to love their fellow-men. But whereas David said 'you ought because the situation demands it', Carol's view was that 'you ought because the situation *and God* demand it'.

*   *   *

Christmas was one of the few times Dave agreed to go to church with the rest of the family. His mother always went when there was anything special, and this time Carol's Sunday School class was to be singing round the Christmas tree. Mrs. Harvey always liked that. And however unsentimental Dave claimed to be from January to November, his stony heart did melt just a little bit in December. He didn't feel 'right' if he didn't go to church at least once during the Christmas season. It meant he could eat his turkey with a clear conscience.

This time, however—was he getting older, or perhaps just more rebellious?—this time he did start to question things a bit. For one thing he found it hard to pray anything when he sat down in the church. So he just bowed his head for a suitable length of time. But somehow he didn't feel good about it. It seemed hypocritical. He took more notice of the readings, too. This year they seemed even more far-fetched. Do people really swallow it all? Seemed unlikely to Dave. And all this fuss over a baby. . . . He felt he'd outgrown it. Mind you, the big congregation would at least boost the collection. . . . Then came that third carol, 'Hark! the herald-angels sing'. Now, he'd sung that many times before—good tune, and very Christmasy. But one of the lines really grated on his better sensitivity. It went—

> 'Peace on earth and mercy mild,
> God and sinners reconciled.'

God. And sinners. Is that all there is in the world? Their vicar was always going on about sin. But here it was turning up in a Christmas carol, of all places.

It's true that many hymns aren't merely paeans of praise to an Almighty God, but are rather expressions of man's sinful, inadequate state. The

33

descriptions of man as 'passive clay', 'the meanest vessel', and even 'poor worm' put into our tuneful mouths by the hymn-writers are not flattering to the humblest of our species. And look at that verse:

> 'And every virtue we possess,
>   And every conquest won,
>   And every thought of holiness
>   Are His alone.'

Hasn't a fellow an ounce of good in him? Can't he take the credit for anything? This is what seemed so wrong to Dave. He didn't feel as black and sinful as the vicar and St. Paul tried to make out. In fact, he felt fairly O.K.

So do the Humanists feel fairly O.K. They find this Christian concept of 'sin' discrediting to human nature. For the Christian ideas of original sin and Fall of man, they substitute belief in man's original virtue and gradual rising to maturity. The Humanist Garden of Eden possesses a tree of knowledge all right. But often a knowledge only of man's inherent worth and capabilities for self-improvement, an awareness of himself—not, as in the Genesis story, a knowledge of good and evil and an awareness of God. The idea of sin to the Humanist, as to Dave, is distasteful.

Similarly the concept of self-denial, that long-extolled Christian virtue, is considered by Humanists to be a hindrance to the noble cause of mankind's progress. And any thought of drawing aside from the world to communicate with God is scoffed at almost before it even enters the mind. This, they believe, only leads ultimately to a greater self-interest, since man becomes un-healthily preoccupied with his own soul. He becomes inhibited, enumerating his sins, and brooding on his misdoings. Instead, he should look at his potential goodness and develop that. Only when an individual is truly happy within himself can he be of use to the community. He cannot be truly happy, says Humanism, if he is obsessed with denying himself things he really wants.

Humanists are optimists. Their hopes for the future rest in man's recognition of his real worth and abilities and capacity for self-improvement. Christians are realists. They have hopes, but they are of a different kind because their grounds are different.

First of all, we should say, in defence of Christianity, that any concentration upon 'sin' or worthlessness is only part of the picture, and a small part. The Humanist argument has become unbalanced. True, it was Jesus who said, 'Who-ever does not take up his cross and follow in My steps, is not worthy of Me' (Matt. 10.38). But a few verses earlier in the same chapter of Matthew's Gospel, we read that we are individually of infinite worth and importance, so much so that even the hairs of our head are all numbered (Matt. 10.30). And although the Apostle Paul said, 'Whatever gain I had I counted as loss for the sake of Christ' (Phil. 3.7), he was also blessed with considerable self-respect, for in the previous verses he enumerated his virtues (which were worthy indeed by contemporary standards)—'If any other man thinks he has reason for confidence in the flesh, I have more'. And he had. But the point was that these, however precious and worthwhile, paled to insignificance in the light of the 'surpassing worth of knowing Christ Jesus my Lord' (Phil. 3.8). In the words of Prof. D. M. Mackay, '. . . from the Christian standpoint, any belittling of man is not merely contrary to the spirit of the Bible, but is sin. In so far as the Humanist is indignant against what he sees as a belittling of man, the Christian is a brother to him.'

The Christian, then, objects to Humanism in the field of ethics on the ground that it is unrealistic as a working philosophy. It has no starting-point, no resources, no limits. Imagine going to buy something you don't want, with no money, only to find the shop is closed when you arrive. You really wasted your time on a fruitless expedition. The downfall of Humanism lies in the fact that its ethical principles are expected to operate in a void.

Humanist ethics have no starting-point. The bus has been running round the block for years. We don't remember getting on it, and can't think why we did. But we're on it, and though century upon century goes by, and men are born and die on it, we have this confidence and hope: the bus will carry on running round the block. Life is meaningless. Life is purposeless. Humanists believe that in the course of time, given suitable conditions and incentive, man's behaviour will improve and his state on earth will get better. They have no concept of creation, as the Christian has. No one has put them 'on the bus'—they're just there. They are left unmoved by the teaching that God made man 'in His own likeness', for a perfect life of communion with Himself, which was broken only by man's disobedience. Their view of life is evolutionary, as we have seen. So, morally, they have no starting-point, no Ten Commandments, no Sermon on the Mount, no 'thus saith the Lord . . .', no God to whom to appeal, no divine example to follow. In the words of H. J. Blackham (*Objections to Humanism*, p. 15): 'There is no supreme exemplar of Humanist ethics, because, on Humanist assumptions, there is no *summum bonum*, no chief end of all action, no far-off crowning event to which all things move and for which all things exist. Instead there are many possibilities, better and worse, and ways of avoiding the worse and realizing and increasing the better. Thus there are many patterns of good living which can be exemplified, and none that is best, or comprehensively or exhaustively good.'

Give a man a good start in life, and he stands a fair chance of behaving in a morally responsible way, says the Humanist. Or, as Barbara Smoker

37

put it, 'Since the behaviour of human beings is determined largely by their environment, a prime human responsibility is to make the environment of all mankind as favourable as possible to individual fulfilment and co-operative achievement.' This view has much to commend it, except that the Humanist is speaking in materialistic and relativistic terms.

It is nothing new for the Christian to say that this won't work. The Humanists must be sick of the Christian finger pointed at the atrocities of Nazi Germany, and at Britain's full prisons. They must be sick, too, of the comment that moving a man from a slum to a new city flat won't alter his way of life. It is, however, unfortunately true. If a man wants to be dirty, untidy, careless, he will be, wherever he is. At the same time, some real gems of humanity are to be found among our slum-dwellers, in back streets which are normally visited only by the police and social workers. Gems of kindness and generosity. Yet we can look in our affluent suburbs and find only the devoted worshippers of the God 'Me and Mine', reliving the jealousies of Jacob, the self-interest of Ananias and Sapphira, the materialism of Demas. There is little evidence for the fact that human nature can be changed by environment. The Humanist, basically, has no reason to refrain from throwing a brick through his neighbour's window, just for the fun of it. It pays him not to do so, and he realizes that if everyone behaved like this life would be chaos indeed. But he has only his environment to appeal to.

The Christian's view is that, having been created by God, his starting-point in life was fellowship with Him. To offend one's neighbour is to offend God, since the law of love is broken, but to put oneself in a right relationship with God has the reverse effect of bettering one's relationship with one's neighbour, and this with no vested self-interest. There is little evidence that countries where Christian beliefs have been overthrown have better moral standards of living.

Secondly, Humanism has no resources. Let us illustrate by another peep at the Harveys' diary.

It was Thursday afternoon and Dave felt great. He hadn't had much lunch. Couldn't eat—in a way he felt quite nervous. It mattered to him so much. Ken from across the road seemed to have been driving for ages, and Dad said that if Dave passed his test he could have the car at the weekend.

There's something about dispensing with 'L' plates that makes you feel like a king. And just now Dave's feelings fluctuated between a glow of anticipated pride, and a dread of failure, and having to go through it all again.

His brain was buzzing with snippets from the Highway Code, advice from friends, and his instructor's last words. . . . He felt so muddled, but he knew he must appear calm and confident. . . .

He combed his hair, glancing quickly at his reflection in the glass door of the office. He set off downstairs, and out into the street. . . .

At 3 o'clock it was over, and Dave, it's true, felt like a king. He flung open the kitchen door at home with a loud 'Guess what—I've passed!' Mrs. Harvey looked up from her baking.

'Well. Isn't that just wonderful! Congratulations! Dad will be pleased.'

Dave hoped so. He had plans for that evening.

At tea he decided to sound out his father's reaction to his little scheme. Dad was jovial and well nourished with roast lamb and potatoes, so Dave chose the right psychological moment.

'Er . . . will you be needing the car tonight, Dad?'

'I knew it. I don't suppose I'll be able to call it my own any more now.' Even so, Dad smiled, secretly proud of his son's success. 'When do you want it?'

'All evening, if possible.'

'Not possible,' said Dad, 'but you can have it for a bit of a spin until half-past-eight. You'll have to be back by then because it's the Bowls A.G.M. and they can't do without a chairman. I must be there no later than 9 o'clock.'

'Carol's coming, so we'll have a watch between us. We'd better get going. . . .'

Carol didn't feel the height of security, despite Dave's assumed air of confidence at the wheel. She was quite glad, therefore, when Dave suggested they should stop at Joe's place for a coffee. He knew Ken was going to be there, but he also hoped to see Judy. He'd looked forward to this all day. Pity Carol was there really—though for some reason Ken seemed to like Carol. Funny, really—Dave didn't think she was Ken's type at all.

They bought a coffee and joined the others. They were soon discussing cars, Dave talking as though he was about to buy one the next day. Never mind. It impressed Judy.

The time passed quickly. Another coffee. A stroll to look at the car, and peer under the bonnet. Dave felt proud. He hoped Judy did, too.

The evening was warm, and casual.

It was nine o'clock when they realized the time.

'Thought you couldn't stay,' said Ken.

'It can't really be that late.'

'It is.'

'What shall we do, Carol?'

Carol didn't know what to say. Dad would be on his way to the meeting now, so there was no point in rushing back.

'May as well stay a bit now,' said Dave. 'We'll only have to sit at home if we go now. Good job Dad was in a good mood tonight. . . .'

Dad's good mood unfortunately came to an abrupt end at ten to nine when there was still no sign of the car, and he had to set off and walk the two miles, arriving late, and delaying the start of the meeting.

He, of all people, should have been there on

time. The meeting went on ages as usual, but he was surprised and extremely annoyed to find Dave only just locking the garage door when he arrived home.

'Where've you been till now?'

'Well, you see...' Dave hesitated. 'Well, we lost sight of the time. You know how it is . . .'

'I don't know how it is. Do you realize . . .?'

Carol broke in now. 'It was after nine when we realized the time, so we thought we may as well——'

'May as well stay out and have a good time. I suppose you've been driving round all evening wearing the car out, using my petrol.'

'No, honestly, Dad.'

'No?'

'No. You see we stopped at Joe's place for a coffee, and then——'

'*Joe's* place? Not that old dump. You don't mean . . .' Dad slammed his file of notes on the table. He'd had a rotten meeting and now this lot.

'And in any case,' he continued, 'why didn't you drive round to pick me up when the meeting was over?' That's a point. They could have done that.

'We just never thought.'

'Never thought? Well. You're not having the car this week-end *at all*, and that's final.'

'Oh, Dad, but . . .' It was Dave's turn to feel angry. 'But you said——'

'I don't care what I said. I've changed my mind.'

'But Mum . . .'

Mrs. Harvey had been fairly silent all this time, making the cocoa. But she wasn't listening to any appeals for sympathy from anyone. 'You should have known better. And as for you, Carol, I'm surprised at *you*. . . .'

'Why me? Why should I get the blame?'

'And don't answer back. . . .'

So it went on, the whole family were bickering like children. Carol cleared off to bed without any supper. Dave went for a walk down the road, giving the front door a hearty slam behind him. He slunk along with his hands in his pockets, and talked to himself.

'Just my luck. I need the car for Saturday. I *need* it. I've promised Judy now. Honestly. What does Dad think I am? I'm not a kid any more. That's just the trouble. He treats me like a child. And Mum's no better. As for Carol, why didn't she remember to look at the time! Trust her to mess things up. . . .'

He kicked a stone. It hit a gate. A cat ran across the pavement. It was quiet now, cool and still. Dave sat on a seat by the bus stop, just to think, just to talk to himself.

'I'll be glad when I leave home. Perhaps get a job away somewhere. I'm sick of the parental eye on everything. Wait till I get a car of my own . . . wish I had it for Saturday . . . nice girl, Judy . . .

how will I tell her? Yes, a job away. Good idea. Everyone's so unreasonable here. It makes you sick.'

*　　　*　　　*

Carol went to her room and switched on the light. She drew the curtains slowly, and fingered her watch as she put it on the dressing table. She felt suddenly alone. And she felt she'd let everyone down. Dave, by not telling him the time; Dad by not going to meet him; Mum by answering her back when she knew she'd failed to live up to the standard expected of her. She had let herself down too, because she had taken her share in the row, and she had thought she was learning control over her temper. And not just herself . . . God. As Carol thought of God, she began to talk to Him.

'Oh, God, I'm sorry. I hate all this. I hate myself. I don't want to get involved in rows like this. But I can't seem to help it. Please forgive me. . . . Please. . . .'

Carol knew that, once she had started talking to God about it, she would have to put things right between her and the rest of the family. She knew that she must apologize in the morning. But it was the last thing she felt capable of doing just now.

'Oh, God, I know I must say sorry. But I can't. Please help me. I just loathe crawling back to apologize. It's the hardest thing. . . . But You can help me, I know.'

Carol felt calmer now. She had been honest

with God, who knew even her thoughts, and who trusted her as she trusted Him. She knew now that she could be honest and open with the others and apologize. She felt at peace with God, at peace with herself, knowing that tomorrow she would be able to make peace with the rest of the family.

*   *   *

'Humanism teaches that social problems can be effectively tackled by conscious and exclusive reliance on man's intellectual and moral resources,' says Barbara Smoker. Intellectual resources. Moral resources. Think again about Dave and Carol. Not everyone would have reacted like Dave, perhaps. But as he reasoned things out and looked for an answer, he could not see beyond his own life. Everybody was wrong but Dave, so Dave thought. And although many Humanists would not probably react in so self-centred a way, there is in fact nothing to stop them. Intellectual and moral resources presumably vary from person to person, and Dave didn't seem to have a vast supply from which to draw.

Carol, on the other hand, though far from being the model Christian, was able, and found it necessary, to look beyond her own existence and feelings to God, the source of her intellectual and moral resources. As a Christian she could not remain self-contained in her ivory tower. She had to live with other people, and it was only by drawing on her resources in God that she knew she had the strength to put things right. Dave talked to himself. Carol talked to God.

Intellectually, today, it would appear that man has God at his feet. He has found an answer to the creation of the world, or thinks he has. He is on the way to conquering the universe. He can prolong life by medical skill—and, who knows, the day may be coming when he can create life in a test-tube. So now, says the Humanist, man's increased rationality will enable him to tackle social problems with similar success.

Whether or not this is true depends on our definition of a social problem. If we are thinking of famine-stricken lands, the improvement of agriculture and birth-control might be man's answer (though isn't there that sneaking suspicion that, had man not been out to gain for himself in the first place, there might have been a more even distribution of the comforts of this life . . .).

These are not days of peace. Quite the opposite. Hand in hand with man's ability to build homes more comfortable than ever before, to travel faster and further in a day, and to pop up to the moon for a look round, there is this awful cloud of nuclear warfare, possible by the mere pressing of a button. These are frightening days. Although politicians have cried, 'We've never had it so good' and Humanists proclaim, 'What's more, it's bound to get better', the Christian is considerably more realistic. He is not comforted by the cry of the politician, nor blinded to the social problems of his day by the Humanists' claim that man can do it if he tries, that his intellectual and moral resources are sufficient. What were those words of St. Paul?—'I can will what is right but I cannot do it.' 'Draw on your moral and intellectual resources,' replies the Humanist. But this is just the problem. Man doesn't appear to possess a reliable reserve of moral stamina within himself. Everyone is different, with different standards and ambitions. We are surely here presented with a variable morality. How can I be sure that when I am doing what I think is right, I am doing what in fact *is* right? In other words, what is my standard? And in a hundred years' time, will it be a different one?

Carol's standard was the example of Jesus Christ and His teaching. Carol found also that her resources lay in the power of Jesus Christ and His Spirit working through her. She had resources which are available for all. St. Paul met the problem before her . . . 'when I want to do right, evil lies close at hand. For I delight in the law of God, in my inmost self, but I see in my members another law at war with the law of my mind and making me captive to the law of sin which dwells in my members. Wretched man that I am! Who will deliver me from this body of death? Thanks be to God, through Jesus Christ our Lord!'

No starting-point, no resources . . . and no limits.

*　　　*　　　*

Mrs. Harvey suddenly came to. It had been a pretty boring meeting. They usually were, these Parent–Teacher do's. Still, she liked to go, if only to show an interest. The Head's soporific droning did get a bit too much sometimes. At least—that was Mrs. Harvey's opinion. She never expected the meeting to be interesting so she always found it dull. No doubt the Head could have wished for a more lively audience. . . . But then, suddenly she woke out of her stupor. What's that? Was she hearing correctly? . . . abandon the idea of morning prayers in assembly . . . don't read the Bible in Scripture lessons, but just study religion and philosophy very broadly, with no emphasis on Christianity . . . was she hearing correctly?

A dark-suited, well-spoken gentleman rose to his feet. 'Ladies and gentlemen, I do feel that we should endorse this move wholeheartedly. With the present trends in Humanist thinking now being debated in the House of Lords, I do feel that we should no longer impose a religious view on our children, but rather leave the matter of belief entirely up to them. . . .'

Oh, but this is terrible, thought Mrs. Harvey. I mean, I don't go to church all that much myself, but I do think our young people should be given a chance to know all about Christianity, or how are they to know what to believe? No wonder there's so much crime and corruption among our teen-agers. Honestly, I don't know what this country is coming to. . . .

The debate was a long and hot one. In fact no conclusion was reached, and it was decided to hold an open meeting on the subject in a few weeks. They'd not had such a lively discussion for years, so they might as well make the most of it.

Mrs. Harvey obviously felt that a knowledge of Christianity should affect one's behaviour, and the lack of it would result in crime and the rest. Teenagers get it in the neck these days—drugs, violence, free love. . . . But Dave did not fit this category, nor did Carol. Mrs. Harvey no doubt prided herself on their good upbringing. The point is, however, whether they would come into this group, given the opportunity. Would there be anything to stop them?

What about Carol? If Pete, the lad she'd give anything to go out with, asked her to The Dive and then, after a good time, to stay out all night with him—would she? Well, although Christians are not perfect, and do make mistakes, I think you would be as surprised as I would if Carol said 'yes'. You see, for Carol, there's a right and a wrong. And this is wrong. Why? Not merely because her mother would be shocked; not merely because decent people don't do that sort of thing (after all, that isn't true). But it's wrong for Carol for much deeper reasons than these. Wrong, because it would hurt her family, and perhaps Pete too, and this was against Jesus' teaching that we should love our neighbour rather than ourselves, and against the Fifth Commandment 'honour your father and mother'. Wrong, because the New Testament talks about this kind of love within the context of marriage, and to behave otherwise is to contravene God's law. Wrong, because it would be acting in disregard for the possible consequences, in response to a whim of passion for self-gratification, and the New Testament deplores this kind of attitude. Why? What does the New Testament say? A great deal about living. It's a lot more practical than a lot of people realize! Look, for example, at one of Paul's letters—his Epistle to the Galatians. Don't we feel a twinge of conscience or even shame, when we measure our life by this standard? Paul says: 'I advise you to obey only the Holy Spirit's instructions. He will tell you where to go and what to do, and then you won't always be doing the wrong things your evil nature wants you to. For we naturally love to do evil things that are just the opposite from the things that the Holy Spirit tells us to do; and the good things we want to do when the Spirit has His way are just the opposite of our natural desires. These two forces within us are constantly fighting each other to win control over us, and our wishes are never free from their pressures. . . . But when you follow your own wrong inclinations your lives will produce these evil results: impure thoughts; eagerness for lustful pleasure; idolatry, spiritism (that is, encouraging the activity of demons); hatred and fighting; jealousy and anger; constant effort to get the best for yourself; complaints and criticisms, the feeling that everyone else is wrong except those in your own little group; and there will be wrong doctrine, envy, murder, drunkenness, wild parties and all that sort of thing. . . . But when the Holy Spirit controls our lives He will produce this kind of fruit in us: love, joy, peace, patience, kindness, goodness, faithfulness, gentleness and self-control . . . if we are now living by the Holy Spirit's power, let us follow the Holy Spirit's leading in every part of our lives. Then we won't need to look for honour and popularity, which lead to jealousy and hard feelings.' (Galatians 5.16–26 from *Living Letters*.)

We might read that and feel that it is very restricting to be a Christian. After all, isn't Dave better off in the end? If he finally decides to reject God and the Bible altogether, can't he really do what he likes? Surely this must lead to a less inhibited, happier kind of life. It doesn't mean he'll go around bashing people on the head if he wants to. Or does it, if he wants to?

Humanists think not in absolute terms but in relative terms. The words right and wrong have become meaningless as absolutes. 'It all depends what you mean by . . .' is the 'in' phrase. Who, after all, is to say what is the best course of action? Jesus lived a long time ago. Who now is to impose the limits? The Humanist answers 'society'. But that really means 'nobody', since it all depends on what you mean by right and wrong, and as I am different from you, what I mean by the terms is probably not the same as what you mean. So even if we live in the same society, who is right?

There are no sharp edges to the field of Humanist ethics. No barbed wire fence to preserve morality. You can wander in and out as you please. There are no restrictions, no limits. Nobody 'owns' the field any more, and nobody says how you're to use it. Take it or leave it. It's entirely up to you.

At least—that's how it seems at first sight. For Humanists do believe in caring for people, and they do recognize that moral chaos would be the destination of uncontrolled man, so they advocate self-control. But who can blame a chap for turning round and saying, 'I don't feel like it', or 'Why should I?' What then is the answer? 'You must'?—on what grounds?

Today it is fashionable to rebel against authority. It is fashionable to depart from tradition, to ignore long-accepted dogma. Hence the widespread applause for op-, pop- and psychedelic art. Hence the ready market for the most off-beat clothes. Hence the admiration for the pop star who most drastically throws over convention. You can get away with anything—except compliance with convention and tradition. That doesn't normally set you on the road to what they call 'the top'. And Humanism allows for the same freedom in the field of morality and reflects the mood of the age. God is dead. Good—now we can do what we like.

Behaviour, however, imposes its own limits. There's no smoke without fire, as they say. Irresponsible sexual behaviour carries its own consequences. The only trouble is they often aren't carefully enough calculated beforehand. The police are surprised when a burglar walks in and confesses his crime. Why doesn't he keep away? Because he can't live with his guilt. He becomes mentally weary of its burden, and he hadn't bargained for that.

Christianity, however, says that someone has already worked out a code of living for us one that is operable in all societies, in all ages, with an answer for individual failure. St. Paul even calls it freedom—'not freedom to do wrong, but freedom to love and serve each other' (Gal. 5.13). How does an imposed morality become freedom? 'Love God and do what you like' once said St. Augustine. A paradox? But it is true. Christians no longer sit debating how far they can wander outside the field, and how they would cope with the consequences. The fence is up. So they can get on and enjoy themselves inside, knowing that the owner of the field is well and truly in charge of what happens.

Dave felt he had arrived when he was told he had passed his driving test. At last he can go where he likes and when. At last he is no longer dependent on the time and patience of qualified drivers to get him from point A to point B. He's free to look after himself, and this is freedom indeed. But it is only one kind of freedom. Although some restrictions are lifted, there are still limits, and if Dave is to enjoy this new freedom, it's as well if he recognizes them. He cannot now drive all over the road, ignoring the Highway Code and driving at 50 m.p.h. in a 30 m.p.h. area. At least—he can, but he will suffer for it. He has certain freedom, it is true, but he can only enjoy it and exercise it within given limits. He ignores these at his peril.

God has been around longer than you or I, and He knows the dangers to which we lay ourselves open, if we choose our own way, and ignore His advice. He has worked out a code of living. He imposes the limits. We ignore Him at our peril.

Humanism insists that we have not arrived. But it assures us that everything depends on time and scientific advance. These now replace God and His word, respectively. These are the governing factors for a happy future. We repeat, however, that the present day is a frightening one. A day of surgical transplants, and moon chasing; a day of Concordes and colour television. . . . The world is small, and the universe diminishing. Man worships himself and his achievements. He is the great I AM. . . .

No limits? What does it matter? For example, how does it affect medicine? Surely the more we advance the better? Suddenly, however, man finds himself on the edge of a precipice, and the ground may not bear his weight, so great is the power he is holding. A man's personality can be changed by leucotomy. His decisions could be governed by planting electrodes in his brain and pressing a controlling button. (At least, experiments conducted on the brains of monkeys, at Yale University, demonstrate this frightening possibility.) Even the point of death is no longer certain because of medical skill to resuscitate the heart . . . necessitating serious discussions between clergy, politicians and doctors on the question of heart transplants.

What does it matter to have no limits? It matters a great deal more than we realize from the security and warmth of our comfortable homes. It matters that there is a right and a wrong. It matters that God who has calculated the consequences, and set down the guiding principle, should be consulted. Without Him, we become (to use one of Prof. D. M. Mackay's phrases) 'ethically anchorless'. To quote some words of the late Sir Winston Churchill, 'The power of man has grown in every sphere except over himself.' The improvement of environment, the increase of rationality, the advance of science do not guarantee more thoughtful behaviour, more acceptable morality. But, says the Christian, belief in God and acceptance of His standards does provide man with an anchor in life, an authority for behaviour and, in fact, a true freedom and ability to overcome the tension between self-interest and social obligation which is the inevitable personal consequence of faith in the Humanistic credo. It is worth taking note of Jesus' own words in the Sermon on the Mount, which have proved themselves time and time again in the lives of His followers, throughout the ages: 'All who listen to My instructions and follow them are wise, like a man who builds his house on solid rock. Though the rain comes in torrents, and the floods rise, and the storm winds beat against his house, it won't collapse, for it is built on rock. But those who hear My instructions and ignore them are foolish, like a man who builds his house on sand. For when the rains and floods come, and storm winds beat against his house, it will fall with a mighty crash.'

There is everything in favour of having a starting-point, a reason for living, resources and limits, all found in Jesus Christ. He has given us not merely a code for living, but the power, by living in us, in our thinking, by His Spirit, to obey that code. And it works.

Chapter 5

Will tomorrow be better?

Dave nestled down in his sleeping bag. It was just after ten o'clock, and quite as cold as they'd feared it might be at Easter in the Lake District. Ken was reading. But Dave couldn't read. He couldn't stop thinking.

He'd heard the solemn announcement of the newsreader over his transistor . . . '. . . all three feared dead. A team of mountain rescue workers is battling its way through very difficult conditions and hopes to reach the bodies tonight.'

Dave and Ken had had a good day in the Langdale Pikes—not very ambitious, but they enjoyed a good tramp, and the feeling of pioneering most easily acquired in the mountains. Yet it was there that these three young men, two Cambridge undergraduates and an accountant friend, had had this climbing accident. And it was all so near . . . and it made life seem so pointless if you could be snuffed out in a moment.

Pointless. Dave, like the rest of us, lived as though life were permanent; made plans, felt immune to illness and accident. . . . But Dave, like you and I, felt himself pulled up with a jolt sometimes—and this was one of those times. He lay wondering where he was going in life, where anybody was going, where life was going. Was it really all so pointless? If it was it was all too cruel. You could slave all your life at your job, or striving after ambitions, or even achieving a measure of success—but after a few years it could all be forgotten. No one would remember you, or your achievements . . . unless perhaps there was God after all.

Let us illustrate it this way: the show had been running for as long as anyone could remember. A long time for a show. Everybody worked at his part. It was a full-time job, and they got it off to perfection—at least, the actors thought it was perfect. If anything did go wrong, they resolved to put it right the next time. But the car park was empty. The theatre was deserted except for the stage, dark except for the footlights. There was never any applause . . . only uncanny silence. This was not one isolated occasion. This was every night. . . . It had never been any different. Everybody was in the play, you see. There could never be an audience. But as there was no producer either, it didn't really matter how they performed, so long as they did their best. . . .

It was all fairly pointless, really. No producer, no audience. And life, too, is meaningless if there is no God, for He is both producer and audience. Of course, the Humanists would not say this, but this is the logical corner to which they are driven if the existence and life of God are denied. There is a song which goes, 'Up, up and away in my beautiful balloon'. Suppose you were to drift high above everything in that balloon ('The world's a nicer place in my beautiful balloon') and you were accompanied by a Humanist and a Christian. The Humanist might look down on the world, thinking like this: 'It's a nice old world. I wonder where it all came from. I can't imagine what will happen to it in the end. Will it go on for ever like this? What's "for ever" anyway? Everybody buzzing about down there like tiny insects. I suppose that's all they are really. Little creatures in a vast universe. And yet the future depends on them. They may as well enjoy life while they can. It doesn't last long. Make hay while the sun shines, that's my motto. Eat, drink and be merry, for tomorrow we die. It will all turn out all right in the end, whatever the "end" is.'

Then the Christian looks down from the same vantage point and philosophizes about life in the same manner, but in very different terms. 'What a world—mixed up, yet God loves it. When it's good, it's very, very good, but there are too many times when it is horrid. It looks good from up here. God made it. Yes—God. It is all His. He was at the beginning. He is there now, and He will be at the end. Look at everybody busy about their work. And God made them all, and they're each of them individually responsible to Him.

Life's short. Thank God there's a heaven. Thank God we can know Him. Otherwise, what would be the point of it all? I'm glad it's God who will have the last say. . . .'

Man is, by nature, hopeful. If today has been bad he hopes tomorrow will be better. Time is reckoned to be the great healer. And the Humanist is typical in this respect. World wars, crime, cruelty, and industrial strikes all illustrate the fact that man cannot govern his own affairs efficiently and well. But the Humanist remains an optimist in his long-term view of man. On the horizon lie success, perfection, and we must gradually get nearer to it, for man is at the helm, he is in charge of life, and things can only get better. It's a good play with a happy ending, and we're all in it, even if we don't yet know how it will turn out. And if we die, so what? It may be the end for us, but the show won't close down.

Is the implication, then, that the Christian is a pessimist? On the contrary, he too is an optimist, but the grounds of his optimism are different. His hopes for the future rest not in man's potential, but in God. For him death is not the end of it all. For him the end of his life is in God's care, and after physical death his knowledge of God will become complete. Now his knowledge is partial, but then he will know, as he is now known by God, that is, perfectly, completely. The Christian looks at the world and its problems and need, and says, it is God's world, He has provided the answer, the destiny of all things is in His power. He is the key to life. 'He's got the whole world in His hands,' says the old spiritual. . . . 'He's got you and me, brother, in His hands.'

Have you ever thought about the pupose of life; whether, in fact, it has a purpose, whether there is any point in putting anything into this business of living? Imagine a game of soccer, which has no goals, no method of scoring, no rules, no referee, no spectators because, in fact, everybody is playing. They have no home to go to at the end, but that doesn't matter because there is no end, no final whistle. But you can't imagine it, can you? It's absurd. Though you be the most ardent supporter of United, you know it wouldn't do. No final whistle would mean no result, but it is the result which is the purpose of the game. You play to win. You win by scoring goals, and you only score goals by a knowledge of the game, and a wise use of skill, ability and stamina, to beat the opponent. This is what makes the ninety minutes' tearing around meaningful, worthwhile, purposeful. The Humanists urge us to increase our knowledge of the game, our skill, ability and stamina—but for no ultimate purpose, other than the betterment of our lot. St. Paul, however, saw a different purpose in it all. When he became a Christian, his life took on a new dimension, and his outlook and aims were changed. 'Whatever gain I had I counted as loss for the sake of Christ . . . that I may gain Christ, that I may know Him and the power of His resurrection, and may share His sufferings. . . . Not that I have already obtained this, or am already perfect, but I press on to make it my own because Christ Jesus has made me His own. Brethren, I do not consider that I have made it my own, but one thing I do, forgetting what lies behind, and straining forward to what lies ahead, I press on toward the goal for the prize of the upward call of God in Christ Jesus. Let those of us who are mature be thus-minded . . . only let us hold true to what we have attained.'

Achievement, purpose, power, success. . . . A new way of looking at life. This can be ours whatever our social background, academic ability, colour, race or opportunity.

But what about the game you tried to imagine with no goals, no purpose? It is difficult then to measure success. Surely no one seriously thinks of life in those terms? The answer is, sadly, that they do, if they carry Humanism to its logical conclusion. H. J. Blackham, a former president of the British Humanist Association, summed up this objection to Humanism in an essay entitled 'The pointlessness of it all' (*Objections to Christianity*, p. 103 ff.). Humanism is, he says, both too bad to be true and too true to be good. And we agree . . . because it doesn't work, you see. You can't play soccer like that. You can't live like that. You will probably need to read and re-read the following words of Bertrand Russell to realize the real gloom of the human situation through Humanist eyes:

'That man is the product of causes which had no prevision of the end they were achieving; that his origins, his growth, his hopes and fears, his love and his beliefs, are but the outcome of accidental collocations of atoms; that no fire, no heroism, no intensity of thought and feeling, can preserve an individual life beyond the grave; that all the labour of the ages, all the devotion, all the inspiration, all the noon-day brightness of human genius, are destined to extinction in the vast death of the solar system, and that the whole temple of Man's achievement must inevitably be buried beneath the debris of a universe in ruin—all these things, if not quite beyond dispute, are yet so nearly certain, that no philosophy which rejects them can hope to stand. Only within the scaffolding of these truths, only on the firm foundation of unyielding despair, can the soul's habitation henceforth be safely built.'

H. J. Blackham puts it another way, equally gloomy: 'On Humanist assumptions life leads to nothing, and every pretence that it does not is a deceit' (*Objections to Humanism*, p. 116). He describes life not in terms of the play or game, but '. . . if there is a bridge over a gorge which spans only half the distance, and ends in mid-air, and if the bridge is crowded with human-beings pressing on, one after another they fall into the abyss. The bridge leads nowhere, and those who are pressing forward to cross it are going nowhere. It doesn't matter where they think they are going, what preparations for the journey they have made, how much they may be enjoying it all. . . .'

So death becomes the point from which life is viewed. Death, man's inescapable destiny. We are called by the Humanist to live with this philosophy, and this hope that although this life is all, we must still work as individuals and jointly for the improvement of ourselves and our lot. H. J. Blackham's answer to the pointlessness of it all is that we can make something out of life, that its sublime moments make the trivial, the obscure, the base and the brutish worth while.

But life is full of too many 'nowhere men' and it is difficult to persuade them that it's all worth while. Life seems too long for too many people, and any sublime moments become all too quickly engulfed in the black mist of drudgery or despair. Tell the wife bereaved of her husband after only three years of married life that life is worth living if she just presses on, for death is the end; tell the father of four, who is out of work through pit closure, that he must just think of life's sublime moments and it will become tolerable; tell the teenager dying of cancer, that it doesn't matter, that this life is all; tell the fifteen-year-old lad sent to Approved School for repeated theft, whose home has broken up, whose family couldn't care less about him, that his security lies in making something out of life. They'll all turn round in turn and say, 'It's all right for you. But I can't go on living like this if there's nothing round the corner, if there's no answer to my problem, if no one cares. There's nothing to live for any more. . . .' Nothing to live for, that is, unless there is a God and a heaven. In the words of the poet, Browning—

> 'A man's reach should exceed his own grasp,
> or what's a heaven for?'

My seven-year-old nephew asked his mother one day, in all seriousness, 'Mummy, am I real? I mean, how do I know if I'm a character out of a story book?' The answer is a hard one—yes, Stephen, you are real. A few more years of living will convince you of that. You can't pick up the book of your life and read exactly what will happen to you. You must live from day to day, you must learn to understand yourself, your family, your friends. You've got to work: your pulse will throb with the heat of life's day, and, who knows, you may have to sweat out life's night alone. You will have tears, trials, sickness. . . .

What more can we say to this young mind? If we are Humanists, we will go on to say . . . But, Stephen, you will have sublime moments, moments of truth, beauty and realized ideals, moments when the view will catch your breath by its magnificence, moments when your tears will be not for sorrow or frustration, but for the sheer joy of living. These are the times which will make the rest worth while.

The Christian, however, says that there is something beyond our lives and ourselves, some-one to whom to look, whether our life is full of sublime moments or, on the contrary, afflicted by sadness, loneliness or despair. For life, as we know it, is not all we have, for it is only physical life. There is also eternal life, which is spiritual and transcends the material, the temporal. You don't need to look down on the base, brutish and tragic experiences of life from the vantage point of the sublime only to give them meaning and purpose and value. You can look down on every experience, sad or happy, from the vantage point of your knowledge of God, who is beyond our physical existence and can bring us through it. There is a way through life, and that way leads somewhere—to God Himself.

Do you ever think about death? I put this question to a number of young people, and the answer was usually: 'No, I don't think about death very much. I wouldn't like to die young. But we live for the present, don't we . . .?' A few of them admitted to thinking about it when they were young. George, for instance, thought deeply about it when he was at Junior School and the greengrocer across the road died. But now, George is a Christian. He rarely thinks about death, although he drives a car, because he says now both life and death are taken care of by his new master, Jesus Christ. So he, too, lives for the present, takes life as it comes. You will find few Christians who only look forward to a halo and a harp. Christians are very much aware that life is for living—and it's very much easier to live it successfully in the knowledge that both life and death are taken care of.

As I was writing this, I put on the Third Programme to accompany my coffee, only to find not a soothing Mozart slow movement, or lines from the Poet Laureate, but a hair-raising debate about biological warfare, and the possibilities of large-scale destruction of all life by the use of chemicals and gases, used to some extent in the last war. With my four-month-old daughter at my side, it is difficult in the extreme to feel optimistic about life apart from God. I remember the day she was born. As I gazed in natural wonder at the tiny, helpless form, deep asleep in her effort to cope with the laws of gravity, a feeling that was new to me completely overwhelmed me. The thought that she would only die one day made me feel the sharpness of my new, almost cruel, responsibility. The extremes of love and hatred of life began to fight it out in my mind. . . . Until I regained perspective, thought about God again, and realized the truth that no, she had not come into the world to die, but to live. To live—and if she gives that life to God, to live it to the full, and completely. The world is not a tomb. It is a workshop for the Christian, and a launching-pad. . . . But it is not a tomb.

On what do we pin our hopes? Do we really believe that if we were to sail up, up and away in a beautiful balloon, we would find the world a nicer place? If only we could get away from it all, if the wings of a dove were there for the asking? Some try it on L.S.D. for kicks, for the feeling of being transported away. But they come down to earth again all too soon and with too uncomfortable a bump. They have still themselves to live with, and their old situations and relationships to manage. Some live from holiday to holiday—a week on the Costa Brava will put everything right, a taste of the sun is all we need. Some emigrate in hopes of making a better go of things. Students clench their fists in the face of the future—'If only I can get a good degree . . .' and schoolgirls, 'If only I can get into secretarial college, or be accepted for nursing, or at university'. . . . The unmarried long for a wife or husband, and family. The married all too often chafe at the reins.

I heard a young man's view of happiness in a broadcast interview the other week. For him, real happiness lay in the expectation of happiness—a feeling common to both Christians and Humanists alike, except that the definition of the expectation of happiness necessarily differs. A successful business-man, in a similar interview, defined his satisfaction with life in terms of achieving his long-term aim, namely, to get rich. The Humanist pins his hopes on the possibility of human progress. There is nothing beyond the grave, but we can make life more tolerable, more pleasant this side of the grave.

How are we to measure progress? In material terms we have come far, and will travel still further. A poignant commentary on our present standard of living in Britain is afforded by the advert 'Is your central heating stifling you?' We no longer have the effort of even putting coal on the fire, never mind sitting shivering waiting for it to come, and burning logs to help make it last longer. We not only now have central heating, but it stifles us. The creation of new comforts brings new problems to be solved. In the same way, the acknowledgement of human achievement as an end in itself, and worship of the god of mankind's progress, may to some bring new comforts, but they can also stifle man's intelligent attitude to life's new problems. Optimism replaces realism—for a time.

Hector Hawton wrote this (in *The Humanist*, U.S.A., 1951): '. . . it is fashionable at the moment to say that progress is an illusion; but Humanists agree with Julian Huxley that progress is a scientific fact.' Progress in material terms, that is. The programme on the power available to man to win war by using deadly gases is not science fiction any more. It is scientific fact. But it is a frightening fact if there is no accompanying progress in man's ability to master his own selfish whims and self-centredness. Our knowledge of the world has progressed. But what of our knowledge of ourselves?

Man can justly stand back and admire the wonders of scientific achievement, of discovery and invention. He can see how the world works. But when he sees also why it works, and for what purpose, and by what sustaining power, he feels urged to increase his integrity and personal responsibility. The latter qualities do not necessarily accompany knowledge of scientific progress. Knowledge of how the world works is available to the scientist. Knowledge of why is available to everyone, whether he has ten O-levels or not.

We may know a great deal about cars, their engines and bodywork. But if an extra large shiny black Rolls passes by, we soon find ourselves looking in, to catch a glimpse of the important person inside. We wonder who owns it and where it is going. If we had been waiting on the pavement with several hundred others to see the celebrity who was visiting our little town to open a new building, we would feel very pleased with ourselves indeed if the car stopped by us and we were invited to 'hop in'. It was a disappointed Christopher Robin who 'looked for the king but he never came'; he would have been overjoyed if he had not only come, but invited him into the palace. This reminds us of some serious words of Jesus in Revelation chapter 3 : 'Be in earnest then, and turn from your sins. Listen! I stand at the door and knock; if anyone hears My voice and opens the door, I will come into his house and eat with him, and he will eat with Me. To those who win the victory, I will give the right to sit by Me on My throne, just as I have been victorious and now sit by My Father on His throne.' This expresses true happiness and progress. You don't boast merely of being invited to the Palace. You boast of the King coming to see you, personally. But your pride lies not in the fact that you are who you are, but that he is who he is. If the next-door neighbour popped in, you probably wouldn't talk about it. But the King. . . . And you realize that you are in fact important as an individual. So the Christian view is that true progress and happiness is to be found in union with one's Creator, in a life shared with Him. It is this that gives a knowledge of the whys and wherefores of our universe, and a deep knowledge of ourselves, whom He made. This is happiness indeed. And it is happiness which can only increase as we expect still more as our life, uninterrupted by death, progresses into deeper and deeper union and fellowship with our God.

It was one of Dave's comments that made Carol really think one day. 'Eternal life? I don't want to live for ever, thank you very much. I don't mind being dead and gone, so long as I haven't "gone" anywhere, except from the face of this earth.' To his mother, this was a blasphemous way to talk.

'You've got a lot of things to learn in this life, my lad, and the sooner you learn them the better. . . .' But Carol had that awful feeling that although she felt she should violently disagree with Dave, she half admired, half shared his view. It really would save an awful lot of struggle against wrong, temptation, unfulfilled ambition, and boredom, if there was nothing beyond the grave. Then she thought. . . . Yes, and it would have saved Jesus Christ the expense of the cross. Of course we don't want *everlasting* life, if it's like this all the time. A small dose is plenty for anyone. But the eternal life of which the Bible speaks, and which Christians share, is a life of quality, not quantity, a life enriched, not merely prolonged, a life of deep meaning and purpose, the life of God in fact, within the life of man. That, says the Christian, is true progress and hope.

Jesus told a story to illustrate the importance of the spiritual over the material view of progress and success, and to demonstrate the insecurity of life. It is the story recorded in St. Luke's Gospel, chapter 12, about a rich man, who was extremely satisfied with his business, and completely immersed in his own achievements. One day he said, 'I will tear down my barns and build bigger ones, where I will store the grain and all my other goods. Then I will say to myself: lucky man! You have all the good things you need for many years. Take life easy, eat, drink, and enjoy yourself!' But the story goes, God said to him 'You fool! This very night you will have to give up your life; then who will get all these things you have kept for yourself?' And Jesus concluded, 'This is how it is with those who pile up riches for themselves but are not rich in God's sight.' Why did Jesus tell this story? To show that 'a man's true life is not made up of the things he owns, no matter how rich he may be'. The rich man was foolish because he had worked and worked and achieved his aim, but it all came to nothing because his priorities were wrong.

We do not believe with H. J. Blackham that the bridge ends in mid-air, and we all go hurtling over it to our doom, whatever our lives have been on earth. We believe because we read it in the Bible and know its consequences in our experience, that God Himself has bridged the gulf by the death of Jesus Christ on the cross for our sin, and His resurrection is victory over sin and death.

> 'He died that we might be forgiven,
> He died to make us good,
> That we might go at last to heaven
> Saved by His precious blood.'

Those are simple words. You sang them at Sunday School. But they are saying very profound truths that our relationship with God, our relationship with our fellow-men, and our hope for the future, all have been achieved by the death of Jesus Christ. Theologians call this the Atonement. This is our 'bridge' to God, and although our management of affairs is poor, although we are self-centred, imperfect creatures, we can know God through what Jesus Christ, perfect man and perfect God, has done on behalf of both God and man. Now God will no longer look upon us in judgement, but on Jesus Christ. We have been 'covered', as it were, by Him, and instead of looking at our lives, God looks at His, which satisfied Him, and we are able to face a perfect God. The 'nowhere man' becomes God's man, and the man for others. Father Mackenzie, 'writing the sermon that no one will hear, no one comes near,' becomes God's instrument in His plan for the world, and he can face the future with hope, in the knowledge that he is extremely important as an individual.

'All the lonely people' can, in fact, become attached to their Maker if they are prepared to link up with Him. They may still be 'alone', humanly speaking; they may still work in isolated situations; they may still feel cut off from sections of society. But that inner loneliness of the completely introverted personality can be replaced by a companionship which is reliable, not fickle, and present in all circumstances. That question, 'All the lonely people—where do they all come from, where do they all belong?' has an answer. They can, and should, belong not merely to a place or a community but to a living person who is concerned about them. They can belong to God Himself. But belonging means involvement. And too many people are not prepared for that.

Jesus said there are two ways we can travel in life: a broad way, which is easy and more popular, but leading to spiritual death; and a narrow way, seemingly harder, and for that reason less popular, but leading to spiritual life. It is an old proverb which says, 'There is a way, that seems right to a man, but its end is the way of death'. God's way—which doesn't always seem right to men—is the way of life. That is why Christian men and women down the ages have faced physical death fearlessly and with calm fortitude, for their spirits have become all the more enlivened. When St. Paul said that the prospect of departing from this life was far better than living it out on earth, he was not advocating suicide because of despair, but he was emphasizing the Christian hope of spiritual life beyond the grave. We wonder what heaven will be like. We have no real picture of it. But we know that Jesus enjoyed real life in a body resembling His physical one, after death, when He appeared to the disciples and He went to be completely united with God. We can only know that it will be something like that for us.

Do you feel that you can't look forward to heaven? I used to feel this acutely and feel ashamed, as a Christian, that I could only share St. Paul's sentiments very half-heartedly. I felt too young, too enthusiastic about life, too set upon worthwhile ambition, and too much in love with our world to think about heaven too. But it doesn't mean that we have to become morbidly introspective about this business of death. If we are Christians, we possess the life of God, which is eternal, spiritual life. So as the future is taken care of, we can live for the present—except our lives will now have a different quality. And take knowledge of older Christians, who approach death with a deepening joy and serenity in the anticipation of a still closer union with their Creator. And Paul himself was in prison when he wrote to the Philippians.

Kingsley Martin, in his essay 'Is Humanism Utopian?' (*Objections to Humanism*, p. 102), shows how we have failed, yet still insists that the future depends on us. . . . 'We may believe that man progresses not towards Utopia, or perfectibility, but towards a happier and more reasonable society.' Humanism is, he says, an attitude of mind. But Christianity is more than that. Christianity is a life lived by the power and under the direction of God, who made us for Himself, and for perfection. We believe in progress most definitely, but a 'happier and more reasonable society' will only be achieved as each person progresses individually to a life of spiritual maturity.

If you are not sure what you think about it all, try to imagine yourself in the company of a dying friend or bereaved relation. Think what you would say to comfort them. Imagine perhaps what you might feel if you were in their position. That will show you exactly wherein lies your optimism, your hope, your true feelings about life.

Humanists are still at pains to disprove the existence of God. This is significant. I have the feeling that a suspicion perhaps still sneakingly penetrates their minds from time to time—a suspicion that God might be there after all, listening in; that there might be something beyond the grave after all. But they deny it hotly. This too is significant. After all, an army only defends itself in the face of strong opposition.

Chapter 6

What is the truth?

Irene is seventeen. Not well versed in philosophy or perhaps even theology, she talked to me about her quest for truth. A couple of years ago she felt she couldn't understand the purpose of life. She was amazed that other people didn't seem to think about it very much, and she wondered why they seemed to spend all their time working hard to achieve success if it was all going to end in nothing. She felt it was pointless that some people suffer so much to live if there's only death at the end. She felt that money meant nothing, happiness everything; so the ideal must be for everyone to look after himself.

That was a couple of years ago. Irene is a Christian now. Her quest for truth ended in her encounter with Jesus Christ, who said of Himself 'I am the way, the truth and the life'. What difference has this made? Now she talks of a purpose in living, a new standard of values; how marvellous life is meant to be, as God intended it and not as the world makes it out to be. And Irene is still a teenager.

As we look at our world today, we witness the overthrow of absolute standards: there is no absolute truth, absolute virtue, or absolute God any more. This has been brought about gradually by rejection of belief in the Divine, the supernatural. And to think of life in these terms reduces it to the meaninglessness, purposelessness and aimlessness which Irene recognized, and which we all see in contemporary society. So we are driven to ask ourselves, as Irene was, 'What is the point of living? If I'll only die one day, why bother how I live? Why put effort into work, pursue ambition, behave respectably? Why not opt out by suicide, and be done with it all? Or why not in fact, eat, drink and be merry while it lasts?'

This is what we must ask. But an important question remains: what if God really exists? What if we are to listen to His view of life, His answer? What if there is absolute truth after all, and we can know it?

In 1940 Gilbert Murray, a Humanist, made this pertinent remark about Christians: 'The ordinary Christian apologist has almost forgotten to argue that his creed is true; he concentrates so exclusively on arguing that it is a comfort, a source of good life, a psychological necessity.' This is unfortunately the case not only in our debates with agnostics or atheists, but in our Christian pulpits, cathedrals, and in our private lives. If Jesus was right when He said 'I am the truth', it is worth telling people who want to know the truth about life. Lest Humanists lay this same accusation against us, we will now say why our 'creed is true'.

There is a lot of well-meaning sentimentality talked in Christian groups. Sometimes we are persuaded that, if we are not 'full of the joy', we do not possess the key to life; if we are not dying to pray and read our Bible, there is something missing in our experience, or that if we don't talk to every Tom and Harry about his soul's salvation, we haven't 'got what it takes'. Now these are extremes of experience which we all feel from time to time. But they remain experience.

I well remember being told a Christian should never be 'up and down'. What did that person mean? I'm me. Of course I'll be up and down, of course I'll hit the heights and the depths. Because of my temperament, I will always live a life of contrasts in feeling and experience. And perhaps you are like me. But it is for that very reason that I am thankful that Christianity does not rest upon feeling, emotion or experience, but upon fact, and upon the truth about man, his past, present and future, and about God his Maker, Saviour and Guide. This truth is sufficient for 'down' as well as 'up' experiences. It is truth which will bear intellectual scrutiny; it is truth which will survive the attacks of the atheist, or the cold complacency of the apathetic. It is truth, intelligible to the mind of a child, acceptable to the brain of a professor. It is truth.

If the Humanist who thinks we are misguided, brainwashed and deluded, could disprove the fact of the Resurrection of Jesus Christ, we could believe his assessment of our position. We would witness not only the collapse of our own faith, but that of countless millions of others, and a history full of deluded men and women. There is only one thing, though, and that is that I have not yet read any Humanist or other literature or met anyone who has been able satisfactorily to disprove it.

This is not the place to launch a full-scale enquiry into the trustworthiness of the New Testament records—you can investigate it for yourself.*

Nor is it the place for a detailed investigation into the historicity of the Resurrection.†

But think about these facts:

Jesus was crucified—nailed to a cross, and died. He was then buried in the tomb of a wealthy follower, Joseph of Arimathea. The Jews were afraid now they had persuaded the Romans to kill Jesus (afraid—perhaps of His followers, perhaps of Jesus Himself?) and asked for Pilate to place a guard at the entrance of the tomb. Pilate, however, insisted that they should guard it themselves, if they were so worried, so they did. On the third day after the crucifixion, the tomb was empty.

---

* See, e.g., *The New Testament Documents* by Prof. F. F. Bruce (I.V.P.)

† See, e.g, *Man Alive* by Michael Green (I.V.P.); *Who Moved the Stone?* by Frank Morrison (Faber).

There can be no doubt about that. The body had gone. Joseph of Arimathea could not produce it, or he would have done so specially to save the disciples embarrassment and persecution. The tomb could not have been mistaken—three women and Joseph all went to it on the Friday, and it is unlikely that all were mistaken. Could the body have been moved? If the Jews themselves had moved it, they would have produced it to show the fallacy of the disciples' claims about their Lord and Master, and they could have stopped this Christianity, which many of them hated so much, from spreading. But they didn't—on the contrary, many priests in fact believed (Acts 6.7). Nor could the disciples have moved the body because of the Jewish guard, and it is unlikely that they would *all* have testified to the fact, and faced persecution, suffering and death for it, if anyone could have escaped it by producing the body. A large number of people saw Jesus after the Resurrection. It is unlikely that this was a fabricated story—with so many different temperaments and intellects involved. Someone would have spoilt the plan if it were merely made up to impress. In any case, look at the grave-clothes. They were lying just as though the body had vanished from them, still in the shape they were given when wrapped round Jesus. But Jesus Himself had disappeared. If anyone had taken Him away, surely they would have removed Him in His grave-clothes.

The fact is that Jesus was seen alive! If you are still in doubt, investigate it still further for yourself. Read the Gospels and Acts; try to account for the change in the lives of the disciples —Thomas, who did not *want* to believe (John 20.25), Peter, who once denied knowing Jesus to a mere maid (John 18.25), and yet preached so effectively that a great number became Christians on the Day of Pentecost (Acts 2). Think about Paul, a slave to his Jewish upbringing and scholarship, and actively persecuting Christians, until he saw Stephen praying while he was stoned to death; and until he later met Jesus Himself on the road to Damascus.

Why does it matter whether you believe in the Resurrection or not? Why can't we say that Jesus Christ was just a good example, and that His teaching is worth following? Because that position is completely untenable—though many people do not apparently realize it.

You see, if Jesus wasn't who He said He was, He was a deceiver and a liar, and full of self-conceit. If you read the Gospels with the view that Jesus was only a man, do not be surprised if you feel repulsed by many of the things He said and did. Good, kind, respectable men do not behave like that. They do not accept worship, they do not criticize, they do not speak of themselves as the way to God, and the only way. Who was Jesus to call the Pharisees hypocrites? Who was He to throw the money changers out of the

Temple? Who was He to weep over Jerusalem? Who was He to draw men from their jobs to follow Him? Who was *He*?

The answer to this is found in the Resurrection. He was God. He had power over sin and death. This is why He could perform miracles, heal the sick, raise the dead; this is why He could resist temptation, teach with authority, forgive sins. In Him lay the key to life. And He is living now, today, at this very moment of time; and His life is shared by countless thousands of people.

Humanists display a basic misconception about Christianity. They look upon our faith as a risk that we take, a psychological security which we find necessary to make life meaningful, and tolerable. But it is futile to debate in philosophical terms about God's existence. It is an interesting academic exercise, but it brings one little nearer the truth. For Christianity is not a creed or a culture, or even a way of life; it is a Person, it is Jesus Christ, who was man and knew temptation and suffering, who died on our behalf; it is Jesus Christ who is God, and powerful over sin and death and the world.

If you went to a married man and said, 'I don't believe you have a wife', he could reply: 'Well, it's quite possible—and even likely—that I have, as all my meals are cooked for me, the house is tidied, and my socks are darned. Yes, I'm sure I must have a wife.' This might be reasonable evidence, but if you didn't want to accept that argument you could think of plenty of alternative theories. Surely he would say, 'Of course I'm married, didn't you know? Why not come round tonight and meet my wife . . .', and the cooking, tidying and darning would not need to be mentioned—they'd be taken for granted. Similarly, however much you examine the evidence for Christianity, your mind will always throw up alternatives if you don't want to believe it. But when you meet with Jesus Christ, then you don't even stop to argue whether He has made the world and sustains it; you now know the answer to all these things—for you have met the person responsible. Thus the Resurrection of Jesus Christ is the key to our knowledge of the past, present and future of man's existence. The Humanist says the world has evolved by purely natural coincidence, that man is a collection of atoms. The Christian, however, says that the world was created by God, and for Him, and His power over it was demonstrated by Jesus Christ when He quelled the storm on the lake, when He raised to life the dead Lazarus, when He healed the withered hand, the blind, the paralysed, and supremely in the Resurrection of Himself from the dead. Once we realize the truth of the Resurrection these other miracles become not only possible but extremely probable. When a university student graduates with first-class Honours we cease to argue whether he could manage the Eleven Plus. So when Jesus actually came to life again after being dead and buried, we cease to debate whether He could manage to heal the sick.

H. J. Blackham (*Objections to Christianity*, p. 107) has said that 'Humanists are concerned primarily with the truth of the human situation'. But this truth is, he says, too true to be good, so . . . 'let us acknowledge the truth and provide the goodness ourselves, with pride and without hope'. In the light of the Resurrection, however, the Christian must re-word this: 'Christians are concerned with the truth of the human situation. But the Gospel is almost too good to be true. Let us acknowledge the truth, and accept God's answer for our lives, and live it out, without pride but with hope.'

The Resurrection not only provides the answer to the question of God's existence, but also gives the power for living. Jesus is alive, and now lives within the lives of those who receive Him. We fail in the battle to 'provide the goodness ourselves', but we need no longer struggle. God does exist. He does love us, yet He must judge sin. The death and Resurrection of Jesus demonstrates both His love and judgement of sin, and because of this it is possible for us to know forgiveness, and be able to share our lives with Almighty God. 'For me to live is Christ', said Paul, 'and to die is gain.'

And what about the future? Humanism says there is no future apart from man's own achievements. 'Hope thou in Man' is the watch-cry. But this can only lead to despair. If a train is out of order, we don't get on it. Not only would we not reach our destination, but if we were to set off with it in a state of disrepair, the journey would be hazardous if not disastrous.

Humanism offers such a journey through life. But we can pin our hopes and faith on Jesus Christ. He is reliable, and He has proved His power and shown us our destination in the Resurrection. We are able to pray and talk with Him, to know His presence and guidance and power over wrong things in our lives. We can trust His word. He said He would rise from the dead and He did. So when He says He is with us always, even to the end of the world, we believe Him, and when He says the end of time is in His control, we believe that too.

Why then, if the Resurrection is a fact, doesn't everyone believe? Why are there Humanists, agnostics, atheists? Because we are individuals. As we enter our earthly family as individuals, so we enter God's family as individuals. It is a matter of personal response and commitment. It is an encounter with God through Jesus Christ. You can please yourself what you believe, but that will not alter the facts. And you'll only know the Resurrection as a fact when you also know it as an experience, when you have encountered the living Christ. God has stepped into history to show us Himself.

As for the Harvey family. . . . Perhaps Dave will end his quest for truth as Irene did, in an encounter with Jesus Christ. This would change his attitude; this would explain existence, give him a reason and purpose for living. Perhaps he'll think twice about whether or not he is a Humanist after all.

Perhaps Carol will feel more sure of her faith, too, and more eager to defend it and explain it to her friends—encouraging them to seek a meeting with Jesus Christ for themselves, knowing that He really does exist and is alive today.

And Mrs. Harvey? Let's hope she will fall off the fence on the right side, realizing that Christianity involves real commitment and not just well-meaning sentiments, and knowing not only what she believes but why she believes it.

We hope that all three will have the courage to stand for the truth of Christianity in a complacent, apathetic and increasingly atheistic world. And we ask that such courage will be ours.